© Bill Lea

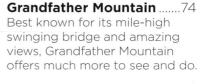

Grandfather Mountain 74
Best known for its mile-high swinging bridge and amazing views, Grandfather Mountain offers much more to see and do.

WNC Agricultural Center 78
Home of the NC Mountain State Fair, the WNC Ag Center hosts many horse and livestock events, conferences, and shows.

Chimney Rock Park 83
This 1000-acre scenic attraction has beautiful views, hiking trails, rock climbing, waterfalls, and many special events.

WNC Air Museum 86
No airplanes under glass or velvet ropes to keep you away when you go back in time to learn the history of these vintage aircraft.

What to See & Do – Attractions 88
From fishing to golfing, rafting to zip lines, go-carts to guided tours, this visual guide to attractions and adventures will help.

CONTENTS

Cover Photo: "High and Mighty"
Our cover photograph of Looking Glass Rock in WNC was taken from 5,500 ft. elevation on the Blue Ridge Parkway by professional photographer Rob Travis. You'll find more of his beautiful art on pages 50-55 and online at RobTravis.com.

Printed in the United States of America   BlueRidgeTravelGuide.com   ISBN: 978-0-578-11829-1

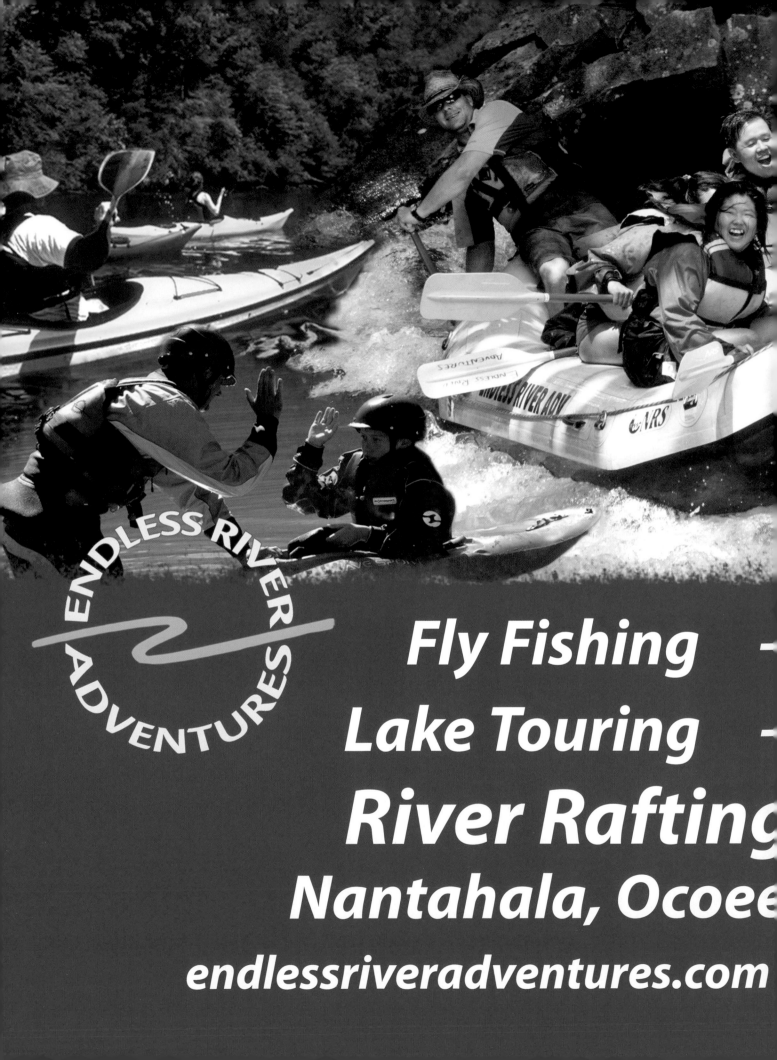

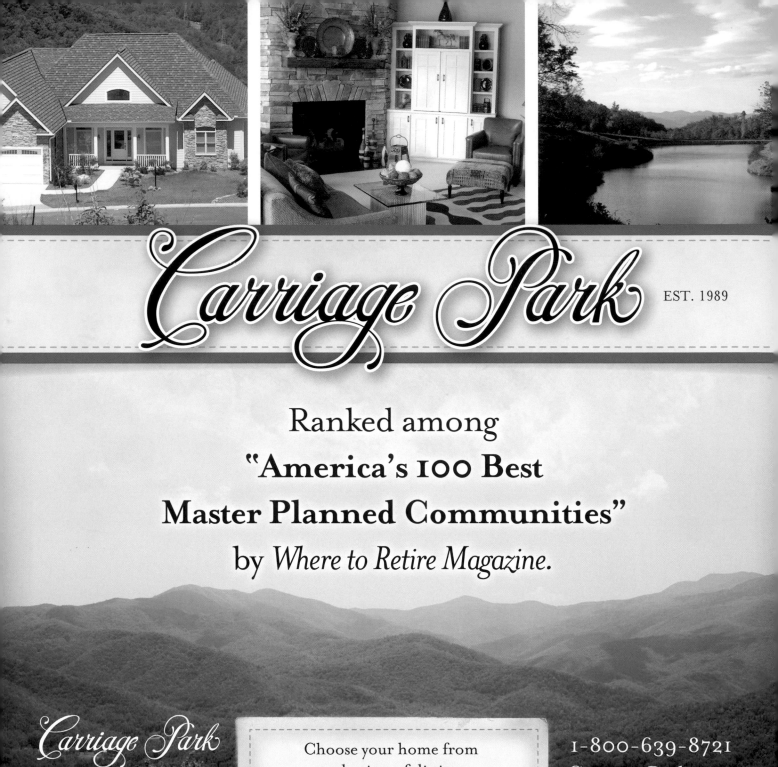

Publisher's Note

As I looked through the photos for this second edition of *Blue Ridge Travel Guide* I was awestruck by their beauty. And when I saw the photo by Rob Travis that we selected for our cover, one word came to mind: ***Glorious!***
I looked up the word 'glorious' and here's what I found:

Glorious - glo·ri·ous [glawr-*ee-uh* s, glohr-] 1. delightful; wonderful; completely enjoyable; 2. conferring glory; 3. full of glory; entitled to great renown; 4. brilliantly beautiful or magnificent; splendid.

What a perfect description of this area, with the beautiful Blue Ridge and Smoky Mountains. They're *delightful* every day. These *wonderful* views are *completely enjoyable* from sunrise to sunset. And because it's so *brilliantly beautiful, magnificent,* and *splendid* I want to make it *renown* by sharing it with others.

The longer I live here, the more I believe it's no accident that we have such an amazing sight to see and enjoy. Someone with a much greater mind and imagination had to create it. And I'm very thankful we are privileged to experience it.

While on the subject of gratitude, I need to thank some wonderful people: First, the photographers, who generously shared their art. I've talked with them, and I know this is no small thing. They spent countless hours and worked hard to capture these amazing photographs.

Second, we must thank the owners and managers of all the bed & breakfast inns, hotels, lodges, resorts, and vacation rental firms who display our book in their guest rooms and vacation properties.

We also owe a special thanks to Ryan & Michelle Owens at Stratatomic.com, who worked days and nights on the layout to meet our printer's deadline.

This book would not exist without our clients. So, to the many business owners who shared in the cost of this edition of *Blue Ridge Travel Guide*, thank you.

I hope you enjoy it. And when you visit our clients, please tell them you learned about their organization through *Blue Ridge Travel Guide*. Thank you!

- Steve Wike, Publisher

Begin Your Journey at
BLUEWOOD PHOTOGRAPHY

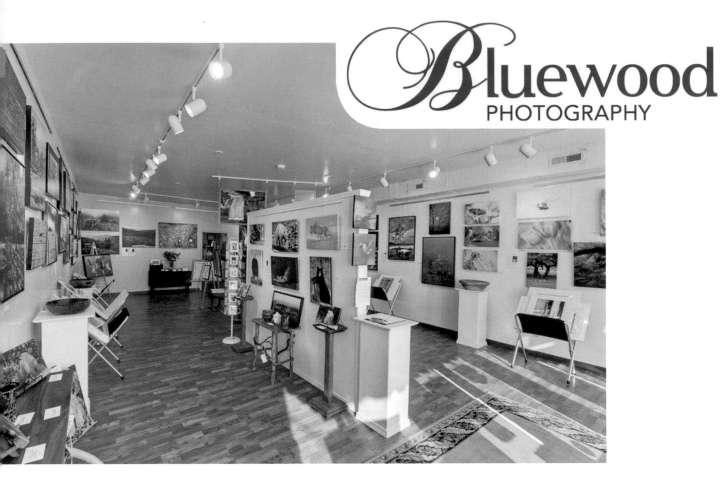

We are happy to reintroduce you to one of our favorite galleries in Western North Carolina – Bluewood Photography. This little jewel is located in the midst of Brevard's shopping and gallery district, and it's near some of the town's best restaurants and shops.

Photographs from Bluewood were so popular in the first edition of Blue Ridge Travel Guide that we asked if we could feature more of their beautiful photos of the Blue Ridge and Great Smoky Mountains in this latest edition. Owner and noted photographer Hal Looney graciously granted permission and submitted some of the most beautiful photographs we've ever seen, including photos of wildlife, mountain vistas, and iconic landmarks.

Many of the photos on the following 23 pages are available at Bluewood Photography, which

is located at 29 West Jordan Street in Brevard, North Carolina. Bluewood Photography has many additional photographs in the gallery that are not featured in our book, including photos by Hal Looney taken on his far-flung travels. Nancy Rotenberg's work is also on display at Bluewood. Prior to her untimely death in 2011, Rotenberg was one of the top women nature photographers in America. Other well-known regional and national artists are also featured.

In addition to the gallery, Bluewood Photography provides printing services to professional and amateur photographers, and photography workshops, classes and in-field photography experiences. Bluewood's friendly, knowledgeable staff is helpful and attentive, and they offer a wealth of information to make your visit there memorable.

Special thanks to these contributors from Bluewood Photography

Bill Lea
Photographer, Teacher, Writer, Wildlife Advocate

Sue Hershey
Fine Art Photographer, Arts Advocate

Bruce Siulinski
Photography, Graphic Design, Custom Framing

Ben Geer Keys
Civic Leader, Fine Art Nature Photographer

Jack Christfield
Photographer, Workshop Leader, Printer

Hannah Davis
Brevard College Student, Photography Intern

Jeff Miller
Fine Art and Architectural Photographer, Printer, Teacher

Ken Voltz
Workshop Leader, Photographer, Gallery Associate

Nancy Rotenberg
Photographer, Writer, Teacher

Hal Looney
Master Printer, Wildlife Photographer, Gallery Owner and Facilitator

Great Horned Owl
Owls often lullaby visitors
and locals to sleep in
Western North Carolina.

© Hal Looney

Cradle of Forestry

The Cradle of Forestry is open from April through November.

© Ken Voltz

Sunrise at Black Balsam

Hiking trails at Black Balsam off the Blue Ridge Parkway provide 360-degree panoramic views.

© Hal Looney

Waterfall in Fall Color
Some waterfalls are so beautiful that their locations are a well-kept secret.

© Bill Lea

Male Cardinal
It's easy to see why red Cardinals are the official state bird of both North Carolina and Virginia.

© Hal Looney

**Barking Tree Frog
in Pitcher Plant**
Tree frogs are sometimes
found in unusual places.

© Hal Looney

Chipmunk
Cute 'critters' are
a common site in
Western North Carolina.

© Hanah Davis

**Carl Sandburg
Barn in Winter**
A beautiful scene at
Connemara, poet
Carl Sandburg's home, in
Flat Rock, North Carolina.

© Jeff Miller

Deer at Mountain Stream
It's not unusual to see whole
families of deer in the mountains
of Western North Carolina.

© Bill Lea

Luck, NC
This 'Little Bit O Luck' made a great photograph.

© Sue Hershey

Davidson River
The Davidson River in Pisgah National Forest provides great fishing, tubing, wading and swimming opportunities.

Ⓒ Hal Looney

Mingus Mill
Water still flows down the millrace to the Mingus Mill near Cherokee, North Carolina.

© Bill Lea

Blue-eyed Bambi
Beautiful deer are found throughout the Blue Ridge and Great Smoky Mountains.

© Bill Lea

Bygone Days
A rusty truck and outbuilding near Highlands, North Carolina.

© Ben Geer Keys

Looking Glass Rock Sunrise
Looking Glass Rock creates a
majestic view every morning.

© Ken Voltz

Hiking the Blue Ridge Parkway
There are numerous hiking trails and camping
options along the Blue Ridge Parkway.

© Hal Looney

Kayaking at
Triple Falls
Triple Falls in the
DuPont State
Forest is a popular
kayaking spot.

20   © Hal Looney

Kayak at DuPont Forest

DuPont State Forest has numerous waterfalls and lakes, with streams crisscrossing over 10,000 acres of recreational land.

© Hal Looney

Barn on Rt. 276
Old barns dot the landscape in Western
North Carolina and create magical settings.

© Bruce Siulinski   BlueRidgeTravelGuide.com

Eastatoe Falls
On private property near Rosman, North Carolina,
Eastatoe Falls bathes 60 feet of solid granite.

© Jack Christfield

Cades Cove
Cades Cove is one of the most beautiful places in the United States for autumn leaf-peeking.

© Bill Lea

Cades Cove Church
Cades Cove is a beautiful tourist attraction in the Great Smoky Mountains.

© Bill Lea

Whitewater Falls
Located near Cashiers, North Carolina, Whitewater Falls drops over 400 feet and has a paved, wheel-chair accessible walkway to the overlook.

© Hal Looney

Back Porch at the Cradle of Forestry

The Cradle of Forestry in the Pisgah National Forest near Brevard, North Carolina, has outstanding exhibits and educational programs.

© Sue Hershey

Pretty Place Chapel

The Pretty Place Chapel at YMCA's Camp Greenville has spectacular sunrise services.

© Bruce Siulinski

Elk in Cataloochee

Many magnificent elk are found in the Cataloochee area of the Great Smoky Mountains.

© Bruce Siulinski

Hooker Falls

Hooker Falls on the Little River in DuPont State Forest drops 12 feet and flows downstream to Cascade Lake.

© Ben Geer Keys

Cataloochee Elk and Turkey

Elk are most easily seen in the early morning or late afternoon.

© Ken Voltz

Barn on Crab Creek
Another incredibly photogenic barn in Western North Carolina.

© Ken Voltz

Brevard White Squirrel
White Squirrels are not unusual in Brevard, North Carolina.

© Jeff Miller

Brevard Courthouse in Snow
Christmas time in historic Brevard, North Carolina.

© Ken Voltz

**Fly Fishing on
the East Fork**
Catch and release
fly fishing is popular
throughout Western
North Carolina.

© Bruce Siulinski

Bear Cub Climbing
Bears are frequently seen in Cades Cove and other desolate mountain spots.

© Bill Lea

Old Barn in the Smoky Mountains
The Blue Ridge and Smoky Mountains have countless photogenic barns waiting for cameras.

© Bill Lea

Dragonfly
Nancy Rotenberg had a gift for turning small things into incredible photographs.

© Nancy Rotenberg

Hiking Cedar Mountain
Guided and self-guided hiking opportunities abound in Western North Carolina.

© Hal Looney

Crib at Cades Cove
Cades Cove is a year-round photographer's dream.

© Bill Lea

Skinny Dip Falls
One of over 200 waterfalls in Western North Carolina, Skinny Dip Falls and swimming hole are located near Sliding Rock and Graveyard Fields.

© Bruce Siulinski

Linn Cove Viaduct
Autumn color at the Linn Cove Viaduct along the Blue Ridge Parkway.

© Dave Allen

Autumn at Dry Falls
Vibrant fall foliage surrounds Dry Falls near Highlands, North Carolina.

© Dave Allen

Dave Allen is a nature and landscape photographer and photography instructor based in the Blue Ridge Mountains of Western North Carolina. His portfolio features a wide range of photography, including landscapes of the Blue Ridge Mountains and Smoky Mountains National Park, waterfalls, wildlife, Blue Ridge Parkway photography, flora and fauna and other related outdoor and nature themes.

Dave is an expert in his field. His photographs have been featured around the world both online and in print. Many of the most respected publications in the photography industry have displayed his work, including *Ouldoor Photographer Magazine*, *National Geographic*, *Shutterbug* and *Digital Photo Pro*.

Dave Allen Photography
828-777-0782
www.daveallenphotography.com
Flickr: http://www.flickr.com/photos/werksmedia/

Flow
Carrick Creek Falls at
Table Rock State Park,
South Carolina.

© Dave Allen

Bridge to Nowhere
Heavy fog covers the
Mile-High Swinging Bridge at
Grandfather Mountain.

© Dave Allen

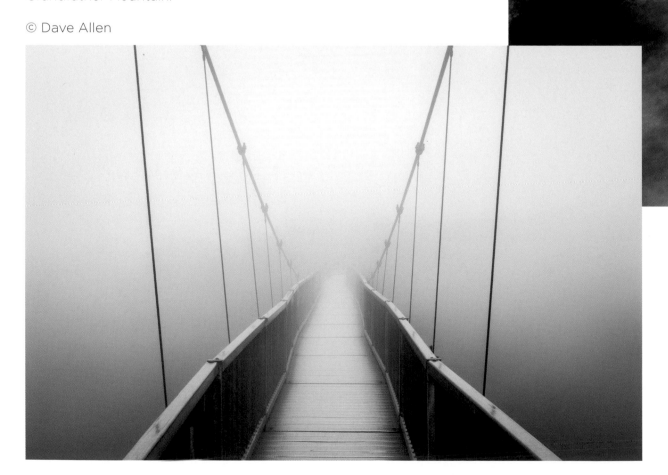

Enduring Craggy
A lone beech tree in the fog at Craggy Gardens near mile-marker 364 on the Blue Ridge Parkway.

© Dave Allen

Highlands Sunrise
Sunrise near Whitesides Mountain in Highlands, North Carolina.

© Dave Allen

Gift of Life
Cascades and moss covered rocks at Roaring Fork in the Great Smoky Mountains National Park.

© Dave Allen

Jane Bald New
Catawba Rhododendron in bloom along the Appalachian Trail near Roan Mountain.

© Dave Allen

Jocassee Gold
A striking sunset over Lake Jocassee in the foothills of Upstate South Carolina.

© Dave Allen

Rapture
A spectacular autumn sunset from
the Blue Ridge Parkway south of
Asheville, North Carolina.

© Dave Allen

Great Blue Yonde
Sunset from the Blue Ridge
Parkway south of Asheville
North Carolina

© Dave Aller

Smoky Mountain Sunrise
A colorful sunrise over the Oconaluftee Valley
in The Great Smoky Mountains National Park.

© Dave Allen

Jim Ruff is an award-winning nature and landscape photographer and a resident of Blowing Rock, North Carolina. He is a retired John Deere engineer who also served on the engineering faculty at Texas A&M University and Department Head at North Carolina State University.

Jim loves nature and the great outdoors and uses photography to share the beauty of our world with others. He transforms nature's glory into stunning images. His interest in photography started in the U.S. Army while stationed near the Korean DMZ. As a cancer-survivor Jim "travels to photograph and photographs to travel." His recent travels include Israel and Jordan, Patagonia, the Atacama Desert and the Amazon River regions of South America.

His work is on display in the Morning Star Gallery in Blowing Rock and The Catch Light Gallery in West Jefferson, North Carolina. Jim's on-line gallery www.jimruff.com includes many of his favorites and he also publishes an on-line photo blog www.BeyondtheSunrise.com and the Facebook photo page Beyond the Sunrise.

Jim Ruff
PO Box 1088, Blowing Rock, North Carolina 28605
jimhruff@gmail.com

Hump Mountain Sunris
A December sunrise illuminate
Hump Mountain (5,587 ft.) i
Avery County, North Carolina

Glade Creek Mill

This replica of Cooper's Mill was completed in 1976 and is located in Babcock State Park, Fayette County, West Virginia.

© Jim Ruff

Apple Barn
Located on The Maze Trail near Bass Lake on the Moses Cone Manor Estate at milepost 294 on the Blue Ridge Parkway near Blowing Rock, North Carolina.

© Jim Ruff

Sunrise Splendor
In early June the Catawba rhododendrons are in peak bloom on Round Bald at Roan Highlands.

© Jim Ruff

Earth Wind & Fire
View of the sun setting over the hills of Tennessee from Whitetop Mountain (5,520 ft.) in southwestern Virginia after a late afternoon thunderstorm moved through the High Country of North Carolina and Virginia.

© Jim Ruff

Craggy Pinnacle Trail

A foggy hike on the Craggy Pinnacle Trail after a spring thunderstorm at Craggy Gardens, milepost 364 on the Blue Ridge Parkway.

© Jim Ruff   47

Winter's Window

The view from the
Appalachian Trail at
Round Bald on Roan
Highlands.

© Jim Ruff

Parkway Sunrise

A brilliant sunrise from the Thunder Hill Overlook
at milepost 290 on the Blue Ridge Parkway.

© Jim Ruff

Duggers
Creek Falls

A small waterfall near
Linville Falls, a short
hike from the Linville
Falls parking lot at
milepost 316 on the
Blue Ridge Parkway.

© Jim Ruff

Rob Travis is a professional photographer based in Transylvania County, North Carolina. His beautiful nature photos have won awards in local, regional and national photography contests, and his work has appeared in many local and national publications. Rob also offers photography classes for all levels of skill and all age groups.

**Rob Travis
Fine Art Photography**
828-883-9088
rob_travis@me.com
www.robtravis.com
www.flickr.com/photos/rob_travis

Rob Travis Fine Art Photography is exhibiting at:

Glass Feather Studio Gallery
www.glassfeather.com
828-885-8457
200 Glass Feather Drive
Brevard/Cedar Mountain, NC 2871

Woolworth Walk
www.woolworthwalk.com
25 Haywood Street
Asheville, NC 28801
Booth 239

Layers of Light on the Blue Ridge Parkway

The rising summer sun on the Blue Ridge Parkway near Brevard, North Carolina, highlights mountain ridges with the lookout tower on Frying Pan Mountain.

© Rob Travis

Dutchman's Breeches

These tiny wildflowers, captured with macro photography equipment and enlarged, are illuminated by morning sunlight on the Mountain-to-Sea trail near Waynesville, North Carolina.

© Rob Travis

Hooker Falls in Autumn

Early autumn light provides interesting color in the reflections at DuPont State Recreational Forest near Cedar Mountain, North Carolina.

© Rob Travis

Connestee Falls
Mountain Laurel growing near the falls along Highway 276 near Brevard, North Carolina.

© Rob Travis

Morning on the Blue Ridge

Rosebay Rhododendron grow along the road with morning light streaming through the mountains and valley near Mount Mitchell State Park in North Carolina.

© Rob Travis

New Beginning

Summer afternoon light streams down through passing rain clouds along the Blue Ridge Parkway near Waynesville, North Carolina.

© Rob Travis

Indigo Bunting

A male Indigo Bunting declares his territory while perched on a Carolina Rhododendron bush at the Glass Feather Studio Gallery in Cedar Mountain, North Carolina.

© Rob Travis

Moonrise Over the Parkway

The full moon rises over a sea of clouds in the valley below, from the Blue Ridge Parkway near Brevard, North Carolina.

© Rob Travis

Sassafras

On a foggy late morning in November, the Sassafras tree leans over the fence and driveway at the Glass Feather Studio Gallery in Cedar Mountain, North Carolina.

© Rob Travis

Ruby-throated Hummer

Ruby-throated hummingbird returns to branches on a small bush at a ranger station in Pisgah National Forest near Brevard, North Carolina.

© Rob Travis

Sunrise on Grassy Ridge Bald

To see the sunrise on Grassy Ridge Bald in the Roan Mountain Highlands, hike along Appalachian Trail near Bakersville, North Carolina.

© Rob Travis

Although Robert Stephens is a relative newcomer to landscape photography, he has always taken photos with camera phones and point-and-shoot cameras on his solo travels (hence the nickname "Solitary Traveler"). In the past couple of years he has developed his skills with digital SLR cameras. What began as a hobby turned into a passion, and his photographs are now on display from Waynesville, North Carolina, to Tybee Island, Georgia. His work has been used by various commercial organizations, and he's publishing his third book about his travels and photography.

Robert Stephens
251-259-8039
http://fineartamerica.com/profiles/1-robert-stephens.html
www.facebook.com/solitarytravelerphotography

SOLITARY TRAVELER PHOTOGRAPHY

Two Seasons In One Day
Snow contrasts with fall colors on Bradley Fork at Smokemont Campground in the Great Smoky Mountains National Park

© Robert Stephens

Golden Rainbow
An unusual "golden rainbow" forms as sunlight reflects off distant rainfall at Waterrock Knob Overlook at Milepost 451 on the Blue Ridge Parkway near Maggie Valley, North Carolina

© Robert Stephens

Winter Drive
A lovely winter scene located on NC Highway 194 between Valle Crucis and Banner Elk, North Carolina.
© Robert Stephens

Little Pigeon River
A lovely fall view of the west prong of the
Little Pigeon River, near Chimney Tops in
Great Smoky Mountains National Park.

© Robert Stephens

Twin Falls
A snowy view of the upper
falls at Linville Falls, located
at milepost 316 on the Blue
Ridge Parkway, 66 miles
north of Asheville.

© Robert Stephens

Roaring Fork Falls

This beautiful, zigzagging waterfall is located on North Carolina Highway 80 in Busick, North Carolina, two miles from the Blue Ridge Parkway, Milepost 345.

© Robert Stephens

Steven McBride is an avid adventurer and photographer whose favorite subjects are landscapes and outdoor activities. He spends much of his time hiking, mountain biking, exploring, and photographing the great outdoors. His photographic journeys for clients have taken him to many locations, including Costa Rica, Mexico, Canada, China, Japan, South Korea, and many islands in the Caribbean. He has photographed coast to coast in the United States, as well as Alaska and Hawaii. Steven's primary work includes photography for a variety of commercial advertising clients such as Cabela's, Wyndham Resorts, Michelin, BF Goodrich, Lowe's, Nantahala Outdoor Center and the Outdoor Industry Association. His editorial assignments have come from many top national and regional publications, including *National Geographic Adventure*, *Backpacker*, *Outside*, *U.S. Airways*, *Men's Journal*, *Blue Ridge Outdoors* and (N.C.) *Our State Magazine*.

Steven's studio is based just north of Asheville, N.C., near Barnardsville. He is a member of ASMP, NAPP and is Wilderness First Responder certified.

Steven McBride Photography, Inc.
828-626-4114
www.stevenmcbride.com

**Claxton Farm in
Buncombe County,
North Carolina**

© Steven McBride

**Fontana Lake,
North Carolina**

© Steven McBride

View from Max Patch Mountain, North Carolina

© Steven McBride

Jones Gap State Park in Upstate South Carolina

© Steven McBride

Autumn Trail Leading to Whitewater Falls, North Carolina

© Steven McBride

Panoramic View from Mount Mitchell, North Carolina, the Highest Mountain East of the Mississippi

© Steven McBride

Kayaking on Lake Santeetlah in Western North Carolina

Butterfly

Snowy Trail in the Black Mountains of Western North Carolina

Joye Ardyn Durham is an award-winning photographer who has been involved in photography for over 45 years and is owner of the Gingko Tree Gallery in Black Mountain, North Carolina. Her images of nature, landscapes and fine art have bee seen worldwide. Joye's photos have been featured in *Our State Magazine*, *WNC Magazine*, *The Wall Street Journal*, *ProNature Photographer*, *View Magazine*, *The Laurel of Asheville*, *Black Mountain News* and many more. She has also worked with Paramount Pictures, including the movie "28 Days" and the television show "Ed", along with Kentucky and North Carolina State Park systems.

Joye is a member of Carolina Nature Photographers Association, Professional Photographers Association, National Association of Photoshop Professionals, and the League of Creative Infrared Photographers. She has taught at the Montreat Conference Center Arts and Sabbath week and has also had over eight years experience teaching photography to both youth and senior adults across the United States. Focal Press has used Joye's photographic knowledge for pre-press book reviews and she is a regularly published photographer for Lensbaby, LLC.

Joye Ardyn Durham
Gingko Tree Gallery
128 Broadway Street
Black Mountain, NC 28711
828-669-7721
www.artistwithcamera.com
www.facebook.com/gtgallery

An infrared image of a barn near the WNC Farmers Market in Asheville

66   © Joye Ardyn Durham

White Trillium blooming in the Blue Ridge Mountains

© Joye Ardyn Durham

Shy young black bear cub hiding under its mother

© Joye Ardyn Durham

Autumn reflections in Lake George

© Joye Ardyn Durham

Blooming spring tulips at the North Carolina Arboretum near Asheville

© Joye Ardyn Durham

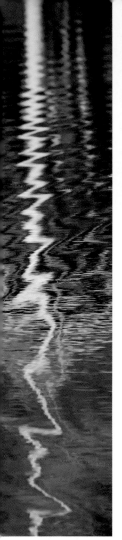

**Standing Rock Falls near
Old Fort, North Carolina**

© Joye Ardyn Durham

**Mature buck in the early
morning frost in the
Great Smoky Mountains
National Park**

© Joye Ardyn Durham

A winters day at Standing Rock Falls

© Joye Ardyn Durham

Southwest Aspens

© Joye Ardyn Durham

Fallen maple leaf in the Great Smoky Mountains National Park

© Joye Ardyn Durham

Spider web on a Catawba Rhododendron near Mt. Mitchell State Park

BlueRidgeTravelGuide.com

Catawba rhododendron blooming around a dead tree at sunset at Grandfather Mountain State Park

© Joye Ardyn Durham

GRANDFATHER MOUNTAIN
Wonders Never Cease

Whether you come for Grandfather Mountain's pristinely protected wildlife or for its tranquil, sweeping vistas, you'll discover a place that's unparalleled in its ability to rejuvenate mind and body.

Rising 5,946 feet above the rugged landscape of northwest North Carolina, the mountain attraction is recognized by the United Nations as one of the world's most environmentally diverse nature preserves. And no wonder – these slopes are full of rare and endangered species found few other places on Earth.

Suspended a mile above sea level and 80 feet above the ground, the Mile High Swinging Bridge is a highlight of every visit. A trek across the suspension bridge rewards the courageous with 360-degree panoramic views of the surrounding mountains.

Behind the Scenes Tours of the Animal Habitats offer participants an experience that can't be beat. Those on the tour get to see where the cougars and otters sleep overnight, meet black bears that are not commonly on display, learn the ins and outs of what it takes to care for the animals year-round, observe a training session and learn why the animals call Grandfather Mountain home. They are offered on weekends April - October for an additional price.

Photo by Skip Sickler

The Mile High Swinging Bridge celebrated its 60th Anniversary in September 2012. This marvel has created memories for millions of visitors, seen its fair share of celebrities and experienced some of the most incredible weather in the state. Dedicated September 2, 1952, the bridge was constructed with wooden floor boards. In 1999 the wood was replaced with steel – a step to make maintenance much easier.   Photo by Helen Moss Davis

With a setting very reminiscent of Scotland, the Grandfather Mountain Highland Games are considered the grandest in the country. Set the second full weekend in July each year, the Games have something for everyone - dancing, food, heavy athletics, track and field events, sheep herding, appalachian music, celtic music, storytelling, and the list goes on.

Photo by
Helen Moss Davis

Any time you visit Grandfather Mountain you will enjoy the breathtaking scenery and entertaining animals, but tag along with a staff naturalist and you'll take away a much greater understanding of what you have seen and a much deeper appreciation of how rare and wonderful this Mountain truly is. Programs are offered to groups or individuals and a 1 p.m. program is offered daily and at no additional charge from June-August.

Photo by
Helen Moss Davis

In June Rhododendron is abundant all across Grandfather Mountain, from MacRae Meadows at 4,300 feet in elevation to MacRae Peak at 5,939 feet in elevation. The plant grows in successive elevation and can be enjoyed for a long amount of time. The Mountain's education staff also offers guided walks in early June that focus on this showy plant.   Photo by Helen Moss Davis

Grandfather Mountain offers two overlooks into the black bear habitats. Mildred the Bear was Grandfather Mountain's first bear and "the nicest bear there has ever been according to Hugh Mortc Although Mildred passed away in 1993 at the age of 26, her legacy forever remains at Grandfather Mountain, in the state of North Carolina, and in environmental education.

Photo by
Helen Moss Davis

When you visit you'll find a wealth of ways to explore. Grandfather's native wildlife roam seven habitats that bring you eye-to-eye with bears, cougars, otters, eagles and deer. Learn about the nature around you at the museum, or wander the trails. Knowledgeable naturalists will answer all your questions.

Finally, relax over a meal in the restaurant or have your order packed to go so you can picnic any of a hundred scenic spots.

At Grandfather Mountain, every visit brings new meaning to the word "wonder." Come see for yourself. Plan your trip today by calling 800-468-7325 or visit www.grandfather.com.

WESTERN NORTH CAROLINA AGRICULTURAL CENTER

Western North Carolina
Agricultural Center

The WNC Agricultural Center – Where a Way of Life, Comes to Life.

The Western North Carolina Agricultural Center is the home of the North Carolina Mountain State Fair, numerous horse and livestock events, large scale conferences and trade shows.

Events of all sizes are held here because the Western North Carolina Agricultural Center makes every aspect easy.

Got big ideas?
They'll fit perfectly at the WNC Ag Center.

This crown jewel of the North Carolina Department of Agriculture and Consumer Services is thoughtfully placed on an 87-acre, securely fenced-in piece of prime Western North Carolina real estate. Its venues are surrounded by plenty of parking spaces fed by flowing thoroughfares, major freeways and the Asheville Regional Airport. The complex is located in the heart of Western North Carolina just a few minutes from downtown Asheville.

For a calendar of events visit the WNC Agricultural Center website: www.WNCAgCenter.org

For facility rental information
please contact the sales office.

WNC Agricultural Center
1301 Fanning Bridge Road, Fletcher, NC 28732
Phone: 828-687-1414 | Fax: 828-687-9272

EXPLORE PISGAH FOREST ON HORSEBACK

Take a Guided Trail Ride at Pisgah Forest Stable

© Michael Rogers, Transylvania Times

Pisgah Forest Stables has been taking people on fun and safe guided tours for more than 20 years through the beautiful Pisgah Forest.

Ride from one to three hours. You choose the trail – take an easy ride through the backwoods with gentle inclines, or spend more time in the saddle on more challenging trails to see waterfalls and other beautiful views.

For rates, reservations and other information call 828-883-8258.

www.pisgahstables.com

Open Monday-Saturday
April 1st-October 31st

Directions: From the main entrance to Pisgah National Forest at US-64/US-276 take US-276 north for two miles; just past the Ranger Station turn right on Avery Creek Road; proceed two miles to Pisgah Forest Stables. GPS coordinates: N 35 deg 18.5 / W 082 deg 44.73.

Professional guides at Pisgah Forest Stables are insured through the Worldwide Outfitter & Guides Association (WOGA). Pisgah Forest Stables is a member of the North American Association of Pack & Trail Operators, and the North American Horseman's Association.

For whosoever shall call upon the name of the Lord shall be saved. — Romans 10:13

© Michael Rogers, Transylvania Times

Chimney Rock Fall View
© Chuck Hill Photography

Few landscapes in the Southeast compare to the stunning 75-mile view overlooking Lake Lure and the Blue Ridge Foothills from atop towering Chimney Rock. Standing on this ancient rock column more than 1,100 feet above the valley floor, it's natural to be overcome by nature's awesome beauty.

Chimney Rock at Chimney Rock State Park is home to five scenic hiking trails, a 404-foot waterfall featured in The Last of the Mohicans movie, ancient geological features like Devil's Head and the Opera Box, picnicking areas and abundant wildflowers and birds. At 2,480 feet elevation, Exclamation Point has majestic views of rugged cliffs in the 14-mile Hickory Nut Gorge. While these make the Park a spectacular place for hiking, it offers more than what meets the eye.

What you don't expect is the novel way of reaching Chimney Rock's summit. At the end of a 198-foot-long tunnel carved

out of the mountainside, you'll board a modern elevator that zips you up 26 stories to the Chimney level. Upon opening in 1949, after eight tons of dynamite blasted an elevator shaft through solid granite, it was the tallest elevator in the state. It's still known today as one of only a handful in America operating inside a mountain. As an alternative to the elevator, hike up the upgraded Outcroppings trail, known as the Ultimate Stairmaster, for breathtaking (literally) sights. Chimney Rock is sure to elevate not only your view, but your spirit of adventure too.

In the spring, dive into a survival skills workshop on fire and shelter-building, or learn about wild edibles on a summer excursion through Old Growth Forest. Listen to traditional folk music on an instrument dating back 3,000 years played by the Park's featured musician, John Mason. Find your favorite regional handmade craft in one of the gift shops. And explore the Park's diverse scenery while you capture the views with your camera during spring and fall nature photography workshops.

As a premier lookout for leaf peepers only 30-minutes from the Blue Ridge Parkway's milepost 384.7 exit in Asheville, Chimney Rock showcases a kaleidoscope of vibrant fall colors from late October to mid-November. Home to Flock to the Rock every fall, the Park has earned its reputation as a birder's paradise with 130 bird species spotted throughout the year, including Peregrine Falcons, and is on the NC Birding Trail. Auto clubs and motorcycle enthusiasts are drawn here regularly, reminding locals of the legendary sports car hillclimb hosted on the Park's twisting road from the 1950s to mid-90s.

Adventurous visitors, experienced or not, can rock climb year-round with Fox Mountain Guides. Try a taster on weekends or book a longer climbing lesson in advance. And every December, Santa comes to practice climbing down one of the world's tallest natural chimneys before climbing down millions more on Christmas Eve.

Each season brings fun, unique events. Peer into live beehives at Buzz on Bees; watch a sunrise or an outdoor Movie on the Meadows; enjoy a concert at Music on the Mountain; or for the hardcore athlete, Race to the Rock on a 5K run or 25-mile bike ride. Guided and family hikes and educational programs are offered throughout the year.

Kids love the Great Woodland Adventure, featuring handcrafted woodland critters at 13 discovery stations along a 0.6-mile trail. Grady's Animal Discovery Den is home to live animal habitats, such as snakes, turtles and Grady the Groundhog. Feel free to touch the skins and skulls inside. It's no wonder GeoParent recently named Chimney Rock one of the top 5 "best summer activities for families" in North Carolina.

The Park's 404-foot Hickory Nut Falls is one of the highest waterfalls of its kind east of the Mississippi River. The 3/4-mile trail to the bottom might still be closed for repairs due to a recent rockslide, so check its status on the Park website. If so, pullouts along the road just west of Chimney Rock Village offer a great vantage point of the spectacular waterfall.

Hickory Nut Falls
© Steven McBride

Refuel next to the Park entrance at Old Rock Café, a casual diner offering American fare. Relax with a local brew on the outdoor deck overlooking the Rocky Broad River, or enjoy live music on Friday and Saturday evenings in July and October.

Go once and you'll fall in love! Annual Passes are a bargain and include Park discounts and savings at favorite local attractions. Leashed pets are welcome. The Park is open year-round except Thanksgiving and Christmas Days, weather permitting.

For visiting information, admission prices and events, visit chimneyrockpark.com or call 800-277-9611.

WESTERN NORTH CAROLINA AIR MUSEUM

If you remember when airports didn't have fences, you could wash the airplanes for a ride, and when you could walk right up to the flightline and see, touch and smell the excitement, up close and personal... then come back in time to the Western North Carolina Air Museum.

See and touch the airplanes that lifted a generation. The Stearman PT-17, known then as the N2S-4, the Yellow Peril, that introduced World War II (aviators to flight. A 1930's Heath Parasol, the first airplane you could buy in a kit and build yourself, or purchase from the factory ready to fly. The Piper Cub and Aeronca Champ, the staples of every hometown flying patch. They"re all ready to roar at the Western North Carolina Air Museum.

Bring your kids, your camera, and your leather jacket. You can view the airplanes in an hour or so, or spend the afternoon hanger-flying with our friendly, informative staff. We can't guarantee fine weather, but our hanger doors are open rain and shine. And we can't guarantee that we'll be flying on the day you visit, but we do promise to propel your imagination back to the golden age of general aviation. Come for the airplanes. Stay for the memories. There's plenty of both at the Western North Carolina Air Museum.

Visit the Western North Carolina Air Museum website for directions and hours of operation. You are invited to attend the Air Fair weekend each year, the first weekend in June.

www.wncairmuseum.com | 828-698-2482

CUMMINGS COVE GOLF & COUNTRY CLUB

Enjoy see-forever views at award winning par 71 golf course playable for all skill levels. Full service restaurant and lounge.

Eight miles west of Hendersonville on Rt. 64 to Cummings Rd.
Take a photo tour at www.cummingscove.com
828-891-9412 or 800-958-2905

LAUREL RIDGE COUNTRY CLUB

Unequivocally, the best place in Western North Carolina for golfing, tennis, social fun, weddings and special events!

49 Cupp Lane
Waynesville, NC 28786
828-452-0545
www.laurelridgegolf.com

Golf, leisure and an array of accommodations afford a well-deserved reprieve at Maggie Valley Club & Resort. Enjoy a genuine mountain resort experience brimming with color and steeped in history.

Take Hwy 19 towards Maggie Valley. Right at light onto Moody Farm Road...
1819 Country Club Drive, Maggie Valley, NC 28751
828-926-1616 | www.MaggieValleyClub.com

BLUE RIDGE PARKWAY GOLF TRAIL

Golf at a higher level...

Come and play America's newest golf trail featuring championship courses and upscale lodging all along the world famous Blue Ridg Parkway.

In addition to the Blue Ridge Parkway Golf Trail, First Tee Mountain Golf offers golf and lodging packages on many other beautiful courses in the mountains of Western North Carolina and Tennessee.

www.BRPGolfTrail.com | www.firstteemountaingolf.com

Waynesville, North Carolina | Toll-free: 866-650-6644

THE WAYNESVILLE INN
GOLF RESORT & SPA

If you're looking to play an outstanding round of mountain golf, look no further than the three award-winning courses at The Waynesville Inn Golf Resort & Spa. To schedule Tee Times or discuss Tournaments, please contact the Pro Shop or email at golf@thewaynesvilleinn.com.

176 Country Club Drive, Waynesville, NC 28786
828-452-4617 | 800-627-6250
www.thewaynesvilleinn.com

3 Award-Winning Golf Courses

PEARSON'S FALLS

Pearson's Falls is located in the foothills of Western North Carolina off Hwy. 176 between Tryon and Saluda. This wildlife and bird sanctuary is comprised of 268 acres of native forest, granite, spring-fed streams and a moderate 1/4 mile trail to a 90 ft. waterfall. There are over 200 species of rare wildflowers and plants. There are also mosses, lichens, shrubs and trees in this Glen, which is classified as a deciduous climax forest.

March 1-October 31
Mon-Sat. 10:00 a.m.-6:00 p.m.
Sunday, Noon-6:00 p.m.
Gates close at 5:15 p.m.

November 1-December 31 / February 1-28
Mon-Sat. 10:00 a.m.-6:00 p.m.
Sunday, Noon-5:00 p.m.
Gates close at 4:15 p.m.

Thanksgiving & Christmas Day-CLOSED. January-CLOSED.
Adults $5.00, Children (6-12) $1.00, Children under 6 free
Schedule subject to change due to weather, please check our website below.

2748 Pearson's Falls Road, Saluda, NC 28773
www.pearsonsfalls.org | 828-749-3031 | info@pearsonsfalls.org

Over 200 species of rare wildflowers and plants.

Pearson's Falls is owned and maintained by The Tryon Garden Club, a non-profit 501©(3) organization.

CRADLE of FORESTRY
The Birthplace of Forest Conservation
IN AMERICA

The Cradle of Forestry Historic Site and Forest Discovery Center in the Pisgah National Forest offers a variety of unique and authentic experiences including education programs, recreational opportunities, and special events throughout the season. **It is a must see attraction in the area!**

11250 Pisgah Hwy., Pisgah Forest, NC 28768

www.cradleofforestry.com | 828-877-3130

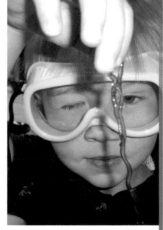

Farmers Market

Western North Carolina's largest selection of fresh, regional produce... and so much more!

570 Brevard Road, Asheville, NC
wncfarmersmarket.org | 828-253-1691

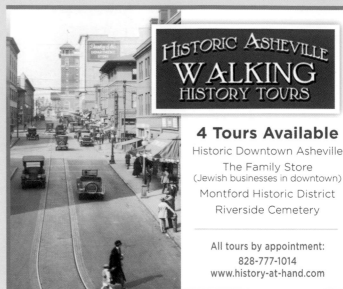
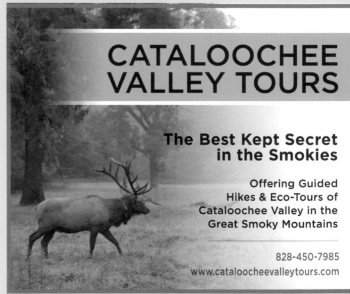

SANDY BOTTOM TRAIL RIDES

Small and Large Groups Welcome, Open Year Round

Sandy Bottom Trail Rides caters to first-time riders, families and children. No age or weight limits. Everyone rides, including the disabled.

1459 Caney Fork Road
Marshall, NC 28753
800-959-3513
www.sandybottomtrailrides.net
www.facebook.com/trailrides

PURA VIDA. ADVENTURES

Pura Vida Adventures invites you to come "Experience the Good Life" with us.

www.pvadventures.com   Open Year Round

Canyoneering
Rock Climbing
Mountain Biking
Hiking
Whitewater Rafting
Kayaking

155 New Hendersonville Hwy., Pisgah Forest, NC
772-579-0005 | contact@pvadventures.com

GOOD CLEAN **FUN**

MOUNTAIN
PLAY LODGE
INDOOR PLAY & PARTY CENTER

3389 **SWEETEN CREEK ROAD**

WWW.**MOUNTAINPLAYLODGE**.COM

828.676.2120
WED-MON **10-6**

For Maps & Information On Scenic Drives Visit
BlueRidgeTravelGuide.com

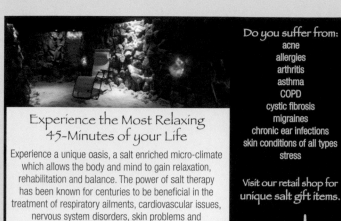

What to See & Do attractions

Where the Most Important Trip on the River is Yours!

Experience the beauty and adventure of whitewater on the Nantahala River. We are family owned and located directly on river. Our specialty is giving economical prices with the very best in personal service, equipment, facilities, and staff. No experience necessary. Guided & unguided trips available March through October. Walk-ins are welcome or call to reserve your adventure. We look forward to seeing you on the river with us.

ADVENTUROUS FAST RIVERS

14690 Nantahala River Hwy 19, West Bryson City, NC 28713
www.nantaharafting.com | 800-GET-RAFT | 828-488-2386

LAKE LURE TOURS

Discover the beauty and charm of Lake Lure.

Relax on one of our covered tour boats while your skipper guides you past local attractions and landmarks such as the locations used in filming the popular Dirty Dancing and the recently restored historic 1927 Lake Lure Inn and Spa. Listen to the legends, and learn about the natural and cultural history of Hickory Nut Gorge, home to Lake Lure, North Carolina.

Tour tickets sold at the Marina. All tickets must be purchased by 4pm. Tickets for the Hourly Tour are sold first come first serve the day of the tour.

2930 Memorial Highway, Lake Lure, NC 28746
LakeLure.com | 877-386-4255 | 828-625-1373

For More Information on What to See & Do Visit
BlueRidgeTravelGuide.com

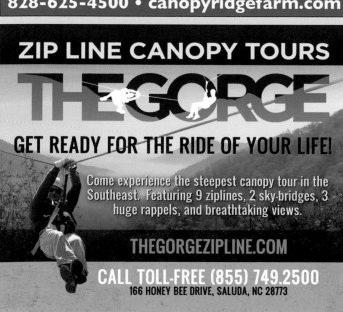

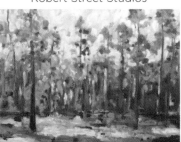
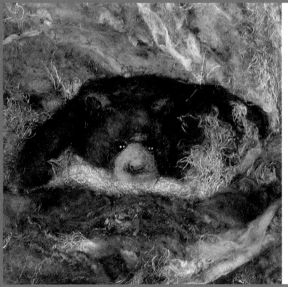

ART & CRAFT galleries

COLIN'S CREATURES
FINE PORCELAIN WOOLLY ANIMALS

Sixty Breeds of 5-1/2" Sheep. Three Nativities and Much More.

Call 828-215-6006 for a studio visit. | www.colinscreatures.com

STUDIO 3

CUSTOM FRAMING & FINE ART

Your Destination for...
Original Handmade Gifts,
Paintings, Prints, Posters, Jewelry,
Ceramics, Wood, and Textiles.

**Fiber Art by Andrea Brewer,
Jewelry by Amy Jacob, Ceramics
by Sarah Jaeger.**

171 Weaverville Hwy., Asheville, NC
828-225-5200 | www.galleryatstudiob.com

KAREN KEIL BROWN FINE ART ORIGINAL PAINTINGS
Ethereal Landscapes Oil/Acrylic

River Arts District - Pink Dog Creative Studio #160, 348 Depot Street,
Asheville NC 28801 and the Asheville Gallery of Art,
16 College Street, Asheville, NC 28801

KKB Fine Art | 828-231-0617
www.karenkbrown.com | kcaabrown@gmail.com

MAINE BOATS BY JOYCE SCHLAPKOHL

Intrigued by light on a variety of subjects, Joyce paints
original oils of landscapes, still life , flowers, people and
animals. Represented at the Asheville Gallery of Art and
the Seven Sisters' Gallery in Black Mountain.

www.joycepaints.com | joyce@joycepaints.com | 828-226-0603

FOLK ART CENTER
Milepost 382 Blue Ridge Parkway, Asheville, NC

The Southern Highland
Craft Guild is an
authorized concessioner
of the National Park
Service, Department of
the interior.

photo © Michael Booher

Home of the Southern Highland Craft Guild,
featuring Allanstand Craft Shop, three exhibition galleries,
special events and craft demonstrations.

828-298-7928 | www.craftguild.org

The 66th ANNUAL CRAFT FAIR of the SOUTHERN HIGHLANDS
U.S. Cellular Center, 87 Haywood St, downtown Asheville, NC
July 18 - 21 and October 17 - 20, 2013

Photo by Stewart Stokes

Showcasing traditional and contemporary crafts made by
juried artists living in the Appalachian mountains, with craft
demonstrations and live mountain music.

828-298-7928 | www.craftguild.org

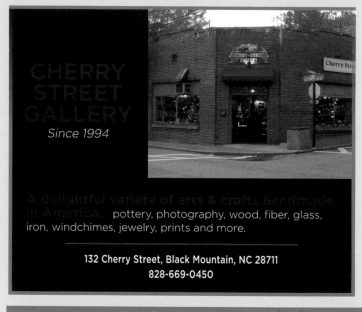

102

ART & CRAFT galleries

WHERE TO SHOP unique boutiques

D.D. Bullwinkel's General Store is reminiscent of an old-fashioned mercantile store with all its warmth and charm, offering unexpected treasures wrapped up in affordable prices and exceptional service. D.D. Bullwinkel's carries casual clothing for men and women, bath & beauty products, gifts, and much more.

50 S. Broad Street, Brevard, NC 28712
828-862-4700 | www.ddbullwinkels.com

FRUGAL BACKPACKER

GEAR UP FOR YOUR BLUE RIDGE ADVENTURES

20-70% OFF Outdoor Gear, Fashion & Footwear

www.frugalbackpacker.com

Accentuates clothing

Dancewear and Clothing
Handmade designer pants, skirts, tops in stretch bamboo, modal, cotton lycra and lace.

By appointment, telephone: 828-298-1921

www.AccentuatesClothing.etsy.com
facebook.com/pages/Accentuates-Clothing/226677100693099

WHITE SQUIRREL SHOPPE

Come sit in our rocking chairs under a 12 foot waterfall and enjoy the 4,000 square foot shop.

- Home accessories
- Amish furniture
- Largest selection of candles in the area
- Bath & Body department
- White Squirrel merchandise department
- Gifts & Collectibles

Like us on Facebook

2 West Main Street, Brevard, NC 28712
www.whitesquirrelshoppe.com | 888-729-7329 | 877-3530

WHERE TO SHOP unique boutiques

WHERE TO SHOP unique boutiques

Come Play At Our Soap Bar!

Discover unusual jewelry, vintage kimono, bags of all sizes, colorful scarves, spicy socks, hats for all heads, handmade soaps, aromatherapy bodycare, cards, funny stickers, beeswax candles and more!

Head to Toe — come to your senses

137 Cherry Street, Black Mountain, NC 28711
828-669-9999 | www.headtoe.com

Bloomfield's
of Flat Rock

Welcome to Bloomfield's of Flat Rock

...Where you will find more than you ever imagined under one roof. Spectacular year-round savings on all your dining and entertaining needs, from bakeware to China, stemware, flatware, pot racks, bath and body products, and a large selection of kitchen gadgets! Name brands include Lenox, Noritake, Spode, Portmeirion, Wedgwood, Johnson Brothers, OXO, Thymes, Nordic Ware, Henckels, and the biggest selection of Fiesta around!

Many out-of-the-ordinary items!

...To beautify your home, indoors and out. Visit our garden center for fountains, unique statuary, bird baths, patio furniture, handmade strawberry jars, and glazed pots galore!

196 McMurray Road, Flat Rock, NC 28731 | Toll-Free 800-754-9239 | Local 828-693-3350 | Bloomfields.com | Open 7 Days 9-6

WHERE TO SHOP

Maggie's
Gifts
Antiques
Furniture

1487 Ozone Drive, Saluda NC 28773 • 828.749.3503
Exit 59 Off I-26 • www.maggiesoldsaludastore.com

Two floors to explore!

Gourmet Coffee Bar
Mochas
Lattes
Espresso

WHERE TO SLEEP

Special thanks to the managers and owners of these businesses who have placed copies of Blue Ridge Travel Guide in their guest rooms, cabins, cottages, vacation homes and resorts...

Bent Creek Lodge
10 Parkway Crescent
Arden, NC 28704
Phone: 828-654-9040

Quality Inn & Suites Biltmore So.
1 Skyline Inn Drive
Arden, NC 28704
Phone: 828 604-0688

1889 White Gate Inn & Cottage
173 E. Chestnut Street
Asheville, NC 28801
Phone: 828-253-2553

1891 Cedar Crest Inn
674 Biltmore Avenue
Asheville, NC 28803
Phone: 828-252-1389

1899 Wright Inn & Carriage House
235 Pearson Drive
Asheville, NC 28801
Phone: 828-251-0789

1900 Inn On Montford
296 Montford Avenue
Asheville, NC 28801
Phone: 828-254-9569

A Bed of Roses
135 Cumberland Avenue
Asheville, NC 28801
Phone: 828-258-8700

Abbington Green B&B
46 Cumberland Circle
Asheville, NC 28801
Phone: 828-251-2454

Albemarle Inn
86 Edgemont Road
Asheville,. NC 28801
Phone: 828-255-0027

Aloft Asheville Downtown
51 Biltmore Avenue
Asheville, NC 28801
Phone: 828-232-2838

Applewood Manor Inn B&B
62 Cumberland Circle
Asheville, NC 28801
Phone: 828-254-2244

Asheville Biltmore Fairfield Inn
11 Rocky Ridge Road
Asheville, NC 28806
Phone: 828-665-4242

Asheville Cabins of Willow Winds
39 Stockwood Road Extension
Asheville, NC 28803
Phone: 828-277-3948

Asheville Cottages, Inc.
29 Asheville Cottage Lane
Asheville, NC 28806
Phone: 828-712-1789

Asheville Courtyard by Marriott
1 Buckstone Place
Asheville, NC 28805
Phone: 828-281-0041

Asheville Seasons B&B Inn
43 Watauga Street
Asheville, NC 28801
Phone: 828-236-9494

Asheville Sleep Inn
1918 Old Haywood Road
Asheville, NC 28806
Phone: 828-670-7600

Asia Bed & Spa
128 Hillside Street
Asheville, NC 28801
Phone: 828-255-0051

At Cumberland Falls B&B Inn
254 Cumberland Avenue
Asheville, NC 28801
Phone: 828-253-4085

Baymont Inn & Suites
204 Hendersonville Road
Asheville, NC 28803
Phone: 828-274-2022

WHERE TO SLEEP

Black Walnut Bed & Breakfast Inn
288 Montford Avenue
Asheville, NC 28801
Phone: 828-254-3878

Brookstone Lodge
4 Roberts Road
Asheville, NC 28803
Phone: 828-398-5888

Carolina Bed & Breakfast
177 Cumberland Avenue
Asheville, NC 28801
Phone: 828-254-3608

Carolina Mornings
44 Merrimon Avenue
Asheville, NC 28801
Phone: 828-398-0712

Chestnut Street Inn
176 East Chestnut Street
Asheville, NC 28801
Phone: 828-285-0705

Corner Oak Manor
53 Saint Dunstans Road
Asheville, NC 28803
Phone: 828-253-3525

Country Inn & Suites
1914 Old Haywood Road
Asheville, NC 28806
Phone: 828-665-9556

Days Inn West Asheville
201 Tunnel Road
Asheville, NC 28805
Phone: 828-252-4000

Doubletree by Hilton - Biltmore
115 Hendersonville Road
Asheville, NC 28803
Phone 828-274-1800

Downtown Inn and Suites
120 Patton Avenue
Asheville, NC 28801
Phone: 828-254-9661

Hill House Bed & Breakfast
120 Hillside Street
Asheville, NC 28801
Phone: 828-232-0345

Holiday Inn Express
1450 Tunnel Road
Asheville, NC 28805
Phone: 828-298-5611

Holiday Inn Hotel & Suites
42 Tunnel Road
Asheville, NC 28805
Phone: 828-225-5550

Marriott Spring Hill Suites
2 Buckstone Place
Asheville, NC 28805
Phone: 828-253-4666

North Lodge On Oakland B&B
84 Oakland Road
Asheville, NC 28801
Phone: 828-252-6433

Princess Anne Hotel
301 East Chestnut Street
Asheville, NC 28801
Phone: 828-258-0986

Ramada Asheville
800 Fairview Road
Asheville, NC 28803
Phone: 828-298-9141

Residences at Biltmore
700 Biltmore Avenue
Asheville, NC 28803
Phone: 828-350-8000

Rodeway Inn Asheville
8 Crowell Road
Asheville, NC 28806
Phone: 828-667-8706

Rodeway Inn at Biltmore Square
9 Wedgefield Drive
Asheville, NC 28806
Phone: 828-670-8800

Sleep Inn Biltmore
117 Hendersonville Road
Asheville, NC 28803
Phone: 828-277-1800

Sourwood Inn
810 Elk Mountain Scenic Highway
Asheville, NC 28804
Phone: 828-255-0690

Super 8 Motel - Asheville
180 Tunnel Road
Asheville, NC 28805
Phone: 828-505-4648

The Lion & The Rose
276 Montford Avenue
Asheville, NC 28801
Phone: 828-255-7673

Whispering Pines Motel
140 Smokey Park Highway
Asheville, NC 28806
Phone: 828-665-1611

Hawk and Ivy Bed & Breakfast
133 N. Fork Road
Barnardsville, NC 28709
Phone: 828-626-3486

Arbor House of Black Mountain
207 Rhododendron Avenue
Black Mountain, NC 28711
Phone: 828-669-9302

Cabin Creek Lodge
1130 Montreat Road
Black Mountain, NC 28711
Phone: 828-669-9177

Inn Around The Corner
109 Church Street
Black Mountain, NC 28711
Phone: 828-669-6005

Monte Vista Hotel
308 W. State Street
Black Mountain, NC 28711
Phone: 828-669-8870

Red Rocker Inn
136 N. Dougherty Street
Black Mountain, NC 28711
Phone: 828-669-5991

The Madison Inn
15 Dixon Drive
Black Mountain, NC 28711
Phone: 828-669-4785

Ash Grove Mountain Cabins
749 E. Fork Road
Brevard, NC 28712
Phone: 828-885-7216

Bradley Creek Falls Lodge
3400 East Fork Road
Brevard, NC 28712
Phone: 828-885-5215

Deer Ridge Property Mgmt.
7737 Greenville Highway
Brevard, NC 28712
Phone: 828-862-8134

Hampton Inn of Brevard
275 Forest Gate Center
Brevard, NC 28768
Phone: 828-883-4800

Holiday Inn Express & Suites
2228 Asheville Highway
Brevard, NC 28712
Phone: 828-862-8900

Red House Inn
266 West Probart Street
Brevard, NC 28712
Phone: 828-884-9349

Rodeway Inn
210 Asheville Highway
Brevard, NC 28712
Phone: 828-862-4200

Sunset Motel
415 South Broad Street
Brevard, NC 28712
Phone: 828-884-9106

The Inn At Brevard
315 East Main Street
Brevard, NC 28712
Phone: 828-884-2105

Days Inn Asheville West
2551 Smoky Park Highway
Candler, NC 28715
Phone: 866-665-2031

Honey Hill Inn & Cabins
2630 Smoky Park Highway
Candler, NC 28715
Phone: 828-633-1110

Mountain Springs Cabins-Chalets
27 Emmas Cove Road
Candler, NC 28715
Phone: 828-665-1004

Nakon Motel
1233 Smoky Park Highway
Candler, NC 28715
Phone: 828-667-4543

Rock Laurel Bed & Breakfast
21 Rock Laurel Lane
Candler, NC 28715
Phone: 828-483-4430

Cold Mountain Cabins
631 Seng Branch Road
Canton, NC 28716
Phone: 828-734-0217

Sassy Goose
1844 Reasonover Road
Cedar Mountain, NC 28718
Phone: 828-966-9493

WHERE TO SLEEP

Carter Lodge on the River
273 Main Street
Chimney Rock, NC 28720
Phone: 828-625-8844

Chimney Rock Inn
3207 Memorial Highway
Chimney Rock, NC 28746
Phone: 828-625-1429

Esmeralda Inn
910 Main Street
Chimney Rock, NC 28720
Phone: 828-625-2999

Evening Shade River Lodge & Cabins
745 Main Street
Chimney Rock, NC 28720
Phone: 828-625-4774

Falls Country Motel
676 Main Street
Chimney Rock, NC 28720
Phone: 828-625-0999

Valley Court Riverside Motel
289 Main Street
Chimney Rock, NC 28720
Phone: 828-625-4166

Inn At Wintersun
1 Wintersun Lane
Fairview, NC 28730
Phone: 828-628-9979

The Cove at Fairview
24 Fairview Road
Fairview, NC 28730
Phone: 828-628-4967

Highland Lake Inn
86 Lily Pad Lane
Flat Rock, NC 28731
Phone: 828-693-6812

Lakemont Cottages
101 Lakemont Drive
Flat Rock, NC 28731
Phone: 828-693-5174

Mill House Lodge
1150 W. Blue Ridge Road
Flat Rock, NC 28731
Phone: 828-693-6077

Mountain Inn & Suites
755 Upward Road
Flat Rock, NC 28731
Phone: 828-692-7772

Mountain Lodge & Conf. Ctr.
42 McMurray Road
Flat Rock, NC 28731
Phone: 828-693-9910

Asheville Airport Fairfield Inn
31 Airport Park Road
Fletcher, NC 28732
Phone: 828-684-1144

EconoLodge Airport
196 Underwood Road
Fletcher, NC 28732
Phone: 828-684-1200

1898 Waverly Inn
783 N. Main Street
Hendersonville, NC 28792
Phone: 828-693-9193

Barker House 1891 B&B
1432 Greenville Highway
Hendersonville, NC 28792
Phone: 828-699-3291

Beehive Cottages
50 Sylvania Drive
Hendersonville, NC 28792
Phone: 828-685-8115

Best Western Hendersonville
105 Sugarloaf Road
Hendersonville, NC 28792
Phone: 828-692-0521

Claddagh Inn
755 N. Main Street
Hendersonville, NC 28792
Phone: 828-693-6737

Cranmore Cottages
208 Millard J Drive
Hendersonville, NC 28739
Phone: 888-868-1779

Echo Mountain Inn
2849 Laurel Park Highway
Hendersonville, NC 28739
Phone: 828-693-9626

Elizabeth Leigh Inn
908 5th Avenue West
Hendersonville, NC 28739
Phone: 828-808-5305

Inn On Church Street
201 3rd Avenue West
Hendersonville, NC 28739
Phone: 828-696-2001

Melange Bed & Breakfast
1230 5th Avenue West
Hendersonville, NC 28739
Phone: 828-697-5253

Mountain Inn & Suites
447 Naples Road
Hendersonville, NC 28792
Phone: 828-684-0040

Mountain Lake Inn & Cottages
801 N. Lakeside Drive
Hendersonville, NC 28739
Phone: 020-092-6269

Pinebrook Manor Inn
2701 Kanuga Road
Hendersonville, NC 28739
Phone: 828-698-2707

Rainbow Motel
924 Greenville Highway
Hendersonville, NC 28792
Phone: 828-692-1150

Ramada Inn
150 Sugarloaf Road
Hendersonville, NC 28792
Phone: 828-697-0006

Red Roof Inn
240 Mitchelle Drive
Hendersonville, NC 28792
Phone: 828-697-1223

Old Edwards Inn
445 Main Street
Highlands, NC 28741
Phone: 828-526-8008

Lagoalinda Inn
333 N. Lakeshore Drive
Lake Junaluska, NC 28745
Phone: 828-456-3620

Lambuth Inn
91 North Lakeshore Drive
Lake Junaluska, NC 28745
Phone: 828-452-2881

Providence Lodge
49 Atkins Loop
Lake Junaluska, NC 28745
828-456-6486

1927 Lake Lure Inn
2771 Memorial Highway
Lake Lure, NC 28746
Phone: 828-625-2525

Exclusive Mountain Properties
110 Church Street
Lake Lure, NC 28746
Phone: 828-287-2106

Four Seasons Cottages & Cabins
113 Boys Camp Road
Lake Lure, NC 28746
Phone: 828-625-8714

Lodge On Lake Lure
361 Charlotte Drive
Lake Lure, NC 28746
Phone: 828-625-2789

Cabins at Seven Foxes
Seven Foxes Lane
Lake Toxaway, NC 28747
Phone: 828-877-6333

Catatoga
1 Indian Creek Drive
Lake Toxaway, NC 28747
Phone: 828-877-6270

Earthshine Mountain Lodge
1600 Golden Road
Lake Toxaway, NC 28747
Phone: 828-862-4207

Greystone Inn
1 Greystone Lane
Lake Toxaway, NC 28747
Phone: 828-966-4700

Lake Toxaway Co. Estates
100 Waterfall Circle
Lake Toxaway, NC 28747
Phone: 828-966-4260

Lake Toxaway Realty Co.
16716 Rosman Highway
Lake Toxaway, NC 28747
Phone: 828-966-4029

Susan Breedlove Properties
16096 Rosman Highway
Lake Toxaway, NC 28747
Phone: 828-966-4026

Wildberry Lodge Bed & Breakfast
135 Potato Branch Road
Leicester, NC 28748
Phone: 828-683-2525

Alamo Motel & Cottages
1485 Soco Road
Maggie Valley, NC 28751
Phone: 828-926-8750

110

WHERE TO SLEEP

Bear Run Log Cabins
1604 Moody Farm Road
Maggie Valley, NC 28751
Phone: 828-926-7566

Brooksong Bed & Breakfast
252 Living Waters Lane
Maggie Valley, NC 28751
Phone: 828-926-5409

Cabins at Twinbrook Resort
230 Twinbrook Lane
Maggie Valley, NC 28751
Phone: 828-926-1388

Castlewood Inn
3695 Soco Road
Maggie Valley, NC 28751
Phone: 828-926-1480

Cataloochee Ranch
119 Ranch Drive
Maggie Valley, NC 28751
Phone: 828-926-1401

Chalet Motel & Apartments
48 Holland Drive
Maggie Valley, NC 28751
Phone: 828-926-2811

Clarketon Motel
1527 Soco Road
Maggie Valley, NC 28751
Phone: 828-926-1110

Country Manner Motel
2474 Soco Road
Maggie Valley, NC 28751
Phone: 828-926-3816

Cozy Corner Motel
3530 Soco Road
Maggie Valley, NC 28751
Phone: 828-926-9711

Creek Wood Village Resort
3340 Soco Road
Maggie Valley, NC 28751
Phone: 828-926-3321

Hearth & Home Inn
3376 Dellwood Road
Maggie Valley, NC 28786
Phone: 828-926-1845

Holiday Motel & Restaurant
3289 Soco Road
Maggie Valley, NC 28751
Phone: 828-926-1186

Jonathan Creek Inn & Creekside Villas
4324 Soco Road
Maggie Valley, NC 28751
Phone: 828-926-1232

Laurel Park Inn
257 Soco Road
Maggie Valley, NC 28751
Phone: 828-926-1700

Maggie Mountain Vacations
213 Soco Road
Maggie Valley, NC 28751
Phone: 828-926-4270

Maggie Valley Creekside Lodge
2716 Soco Road
Maggie Valley, NC 28751
Phone: 828-926-1301

Maggie Valley Inn & Conf. Center
70 Soco Road
Maggie Valley, NC 28751
Phone: 828-926-0201

Meadowlark Motel
2878 Soco Road
Maggie Valley, NC 28751
Phone: 828-926-1717

Mountain Joy Cottages
121 Setzer Cove Road
Maggie Valley, NC 28751
Phone: 828-926-1257

Peppertree Maggie Valley
265 Moody Farm Road
Maggie Valley, NC 28751
Phone: 828-926-3761

Scottish Inn
178 Soco Road
Maggie Valley, NC 28751
Phone: 828-926-9137

Smoky Falls Lodge
2550 Soco Road
Maggie Valley, NC 28751
Phone: 828-734-8792

Tanglewood Motel & Log Cabins
1595 Soco Road
Maggie Valley, NC 28751
Phone: 828-926-1894

Barkwell's Cottages
290 Lance Road
Mills River, NC 28759
Phone: 828-891-8288

Bed & Breakfast on Tiffany Hill
400 Ray Hill Road
Mills River, NC   28759
Phone: 828-290-6080

Aunt Bug's Cabin Rentals
3121 Veterans Blvd.
Pigeon Forge, TN 37863
Phone: 865-908-4948

Key Falls Inn
151 Everett Road
Pisgah Forest, NC 28768
Phone: 828-884-7559

Oaks Bed and Breakfast
339 Greenville Street
Saluda, NC 28773
Phone: 828-749-2000

Orchard Inn
100 Orchard Inn Lane
Saluda, NC 28773
Phone: 828-749-5471

Foxhunt Townhouses
127 Cherokee Trail, Suite B
Sapphire, NC 28774
Phone: 828-743-7667

Hampton Inn & Suites
3245 US Highway 64 East
Sapphire, NC 28774
Phone: 828-743-4545

Andon-Reid Inn Bed & Breakfast
92 Daisy Avenue
Waynesville, NC 28786
Phone: 828-452-3089

Best Western Smoky Mountain Inn
130 Shiloh Trail
Waynesville, NC 28786
Phone: 828-456-4402

Boyd Mountain Log Cabins
445 Boyd Farm Road
Waynesville, NC 28785
Phone: 828-926-1575

Brookside Mountain Mist B&B
142 Country Club Drive
Waynesville, NC   28786
Phone: 828-452-6880

Great Smoky Rentals
50 South Main Street
Waynesville, NC 28786
Phone: 828-452-2700

Inn At Iris Meadows
304 Love Lane
Waynesville, NC 28786
Phone: 828-456-3877

McGovern Property Mgmt.
284 N. Haywood St., Suite B
Waynesville, NC 28786
Phone: 828-452-1519

Oak Park Inn
196 S. Main Street
Waynesville, NC 28786
Phone: 828-456-5328

Parkway Inn
2093 Dellwood Road
Waynesville, NC 28786
Phone: 828-926-1841

Pisgah Inn
Blue Ridge Pkwy. Milepost 408.6
Waynesville, NC 28786
Phone: 828-235-8228

Swag Country Inn
2300 Swag Road
Waynesville, NC 28785
Phone: 828-926-0430

The Old Stone Inn
109 Dolan Road
Waynesville, NC 28786
Phone: 828-456-3333

Waynesville Inn Golf Resort & Spa
176 Country Club Drive
Waynesville, NC 28786
Phone: 828-456-3551

Windover Inn
40 Old Hickory Street
Waynesville, NC 28786
Phone: 828-452-4411

Yellow House
89 Oakview Drive
Waynesville, NC 28786
Phone: 828-452-0991

Dry Ridge Inn
26 Brown Street
Weaverville, NC 28787
Phone: 828-658-3899

Inn On Main Street
88 S. Main Street
Weaverville, NC 28787
Phone: 828-645-4935

The Weller Life®

A life of maintenance-free living, delicious food, lively parties, great friends, security, and all-around peace of mind.

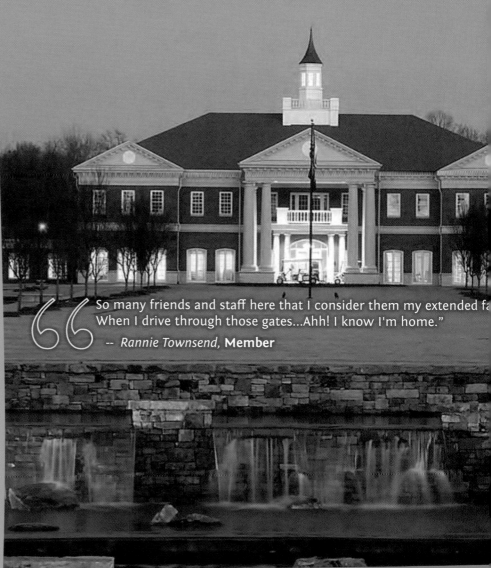

" So many friends and staff here that I consider them my extended fa
When I drive through those gates...Ahh! I know I'm home."
-- *Rannie Townsend,* **Member**

Smiles and Laughter, Gua

10 Fountainview Ter · Gr

Call 864-528-550

Independent Living · Ass

Located on 40 acres, our gated community is designed to better the quality of life for each of our Members.

Afford yourself the opportunity to maintain and enjoy your **independence** for the rest of your life.

Take the daily work out of your life! Spend more time on hobbies, travel, family, friends, and enjoying all the amenities and social life at the community.
– Maintenance-free easy living in a secure, gated community
– Spacious, affordable cottages and apartments
– Innovative wellness program featuring our nationally-acclaimed WAVES and CLIMB programs
– On-site Healthcare and daily gourmet dining

Our partnership with Wake Forest University allows us to provide new exercise programs and more choices promoting independence while aging.
– Aerobics Studio
– Heated Indoor Pool
– Personal Training
– Beauty Salon & Barber Shop
– Variety of exercise & fitness classes and equipment
– Manicures/Pedicures
– Massage Therapies
– Spa Boutique

The Dining Experience
Members enjoy country club-style dining at its finest with full menu service and nightly specials prepared by our Executive Chef. We take great pride in the entire dining experience and work hard each and every day to ensure that your needs are met and your expectations are exceeded.

Health Care if You Need It
Be better, **feel** better, and **live** better with a significantly higher quality of life, independently in your own home.

Security & 24-Hour Staff
We are the reality of security because we have staff on hand 24 hours of EVERY day. When security matters

Longer, Healthier, & Happier Life!

ed. **Come and Tour Now!**

SC 29607 • www.TheCascadesVerdae.com

chedule an appointment

ng • Alzeimer's Care • Skilled Nursing • Wellness

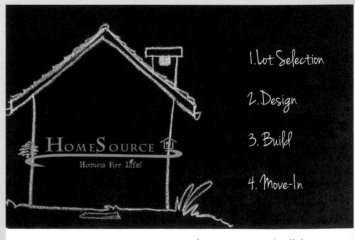

CORK & CLEAVER

The Cork & Cleaver at The Waynesville Inn Golf Resort & Spa is a AAA three-diamond rated steakhouse. It enjoys a great reputation for excellent food and attentive service among locals and travelers alike.

Serving Dinner Tuesday-Saturday Evenings 4:30-9:00 pm.

176 Country Club Drive, Waynesville, NC 28786

828-456-3551 | 800-627-6250

www.thewaynesvilleinn.com

FROGS LEAP PUBLIC HOUSE
A Unique Farm to Fork Experience

Innovative Southern Food with a Local Backbone & Home Grown Libations

A farm-to-table country pub in the heart of historic downtown Waynesville, NC. Frogs Leap Public House is focused on the culture, art, music, wine, beer and especially the food of Western North Carolina.

44 Church Street, Waynesville, NC 28786
828-456-1930 | www.frogsleappublichouse.com

MRS. G & ME RESTAURANT

Chef Linda and her team make everything from scratch – delicious soups, sauces, dressings, even their blackening spice, cajun seasoning, you name it!

Enjoy a great atmosphere, great people and a meal you won't forget.

502 North Main Street, Hendersonville, NC 28792
Reservations Recommended: 828-697-5350

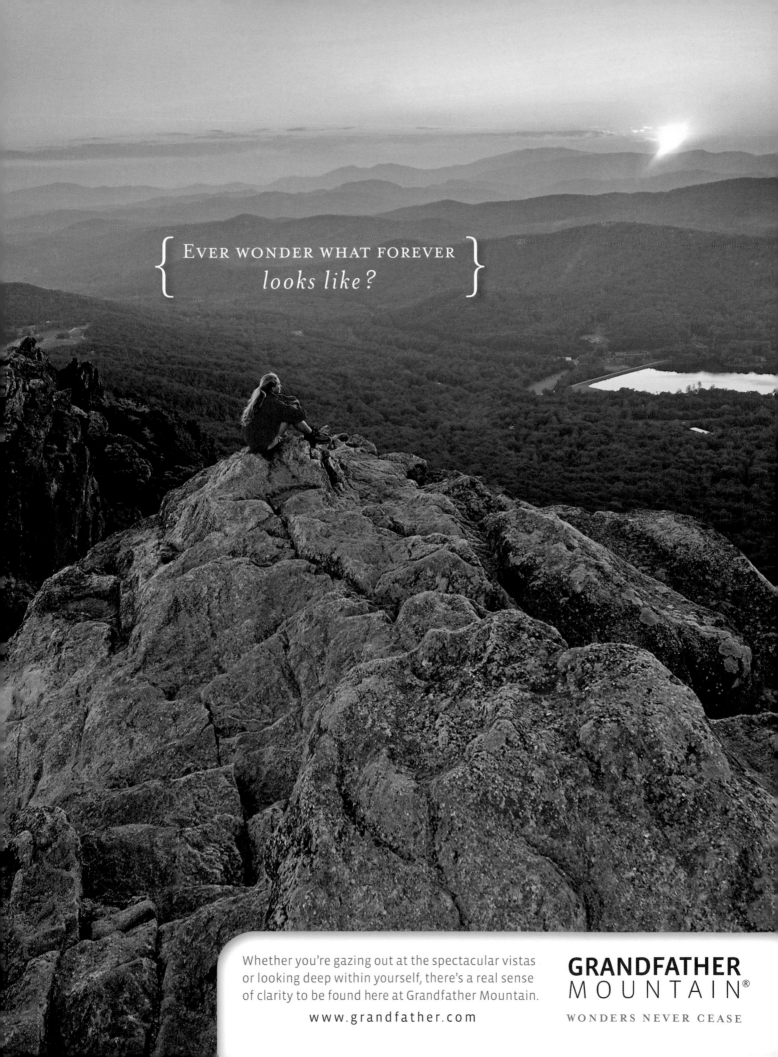

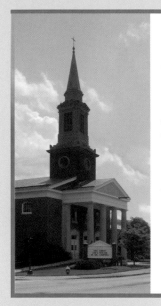

biltmore
BAPTIST CHURCH

Join us Sunday on any of our campuses
and learn about the One who created it all.

ARDEN CAMPUS
Sundays at 9:15 & 11am

35 Clayton Road
Arden, NC
(Exit 37 off I-26)

EAST CAMPUS
Sundays at 11am

74 Riverwood Road
Swannanoa, NC
(On the campus of
Asheville Christian Academy)

FRANKLIN CAMPUS
Coming August 2013

1028 Georgia Road
Franklin, NC
(At the Smoky Mountain Center for the Performing Arts)

Not sure? Get a taste of what to expect by checking out our Online Campus.
Visit BiltmoreBaptist.org/online for on demand video and a live feed of the service.

Arden Campus Worship Center

BiltmoreBaptist.org

Discover The Cove in Asheville, North Carolina, and find renew[al] during life-changing seminars with leading Bible teachers. Or join us for *An Evening at The Cove*, which includes a delicious dinne[r] and concert with a popular Christian artist. From our charming inns and warm hospitality to winding mountain trails, The Cove is designed to help you get away, relax, and hear God's voice.